THE BASIC
SIXTH
Sense

MEGAN D'ANTONIO

To order additional copies of this book, contact:
Xlibris
844-714-8691
www.Xlibris.com
Orders@Xlibris.com

ISBN: Softcover   978-1-6698-2007-9
        Hardcover   978-1-6698-2008-6
        EBook   978-1-6698-2009-3

Print information available on the last page

Rev. date: 04/11/2022

Contents

The Basic Sixth Sense is your minds reasoning towards all form of communication. Becoming more susceptible to the idea of our basic sixth sense you can use become your best self to it to live your best life. The basic sixth sense is important, to sense and re program our reasoning correctly with your other five senses will bring success and change of behaviors that are needed to perform a peaceful life within side oneself and within loved one or those of who we don't get along with by learning to redirecting ourselves as individuals and as a whole.

Without learning there is no understanding. Without understanding there is no comprehension. Without comprehension there is no communication. Without communication there is no relationships. Without relationships there is no connection. Without connection there is no movement. Without movement there is no presence. Without the right presence there is no learning, understanding and communication to the relationships, therefor not being able to connect by our movement we have within ourselves and others.

PART ONE

What is our Basic Sixth Sense

What our Basic Sixth Sense is.

There are crucial moments in life when the "need" of having full understanding within our details that makes us who we are, must be addressed. There are no limitations within what we can become. Limitations only exist from what we have became. There is no limit on what we can become. What we have become is our present. What we have became is in our past. Our past and present only exist in what consist of every moment of everyday. Allowing to have the belief that the ability to have repetitive motion of actions that can change the curse without repetitive behavior being applied, actually exists even when we do not believe it does. Our present are moments that become our past within seconds.

Our present constantly changes, therefore so does our past. If there is belief that our past and present are different, making a change to better our lifestyle will convince us that it's much hard work and prolonging the process will happen. But, every moment within a minute of every day takes that hard work from us, because time allows us to make life easier when we understand there are no limitations to time. Time is infinite, infinite is limitless or endless in space, impossible to measure or calculate. And it all starts with the fact that we are all made up of time and space that's infinite.

How we communicate and what is communicated back to us is like a satellite. We are Earth's satellite living in, earth's space that is surrounded by Earth's time. Life on earth is infinite, how we live our lives on this beautiful planet is limitless. Our possible positive

lifestyle is endless. Nothing can be sparked into something positive without an atom's positive atom charge feeding into a negative atom. From the darkness becomes light. When atoms sense each other to form as molecules they turn into the objects around us. We consist of atoms that form molecules that produce who we are. Everything about us is produced in the form of sensing. Sensing meaning is a form of communication. Communication is the answer to the life we live.

The life we live is formed with what we sense. Our bodies communicate with sensing. We communicate to others, and others communicate to us and we communicate to ourselves. Physical effects from basic five senses allow what our basic sixth sense will process, by sensing what is being communicated in all aspects that communication can occur to us. Every sense and element communicate with each other, our body is just a big lighting rod that just conducts energy. Our mind feeds the energy and gives direction, giving you communication on what can be, and is used in what is comprehended within our basic sixth sense.

Many do consider the possibility of having up to twenty-one different senses. But the twenty-one other senses still find roots to the basic category of the five senses that are traditionally known. While the other senses are branched out from the following known as the sixth sense that stands alone in its own roots of category.

The sense commonly known as just the sixth sense is described as an ability to know something with using intuition and hunch. Intuition meaning, the ability to understand something immediately without the need for conscious reasoning. Hunch the meaning a feeling or guess based on intuition rather than known facts. All of those descriptions are found only in the psychic origins. That does not require genetic ties in eliminating difficulty levels of abilities to perform daily tasks.

We can all live daily individually as a human race without psychic origin abilities, but we cannot live without communication in all of it's forms. What psychic origins bring to those who have a gift is only how they communicate in the form of The Basic Sixth Sense and Basic Five Senses.

Our basic five senses allow us to react readily to impressions that stimulate us. All substances appear to us in a physical form through the currents of electrical impulses throughout our bodies. Every experience we encounter, even emotionally, has an energy. Vision, where the lens in the eyes focuses on light. Rods helps us detect motion that allows us to see in dim light and night. When the retina receives an image that our cornea focuses on through our lens, the image transforms into electrical impulses carried by the optic nerve for us to mentally process what we see.

Taste, Clusters of receptor cells within our taste buds on our tongue. Every taste bud has a pore that opens at the top of the tongue that acts like a filter and catches microscopic molecules and ions within everything that gets put in the mouth.

The molecules and ions travel through the pores to receptor cells inside through vibrations. Smell, we smell when an odor/fragrance stimulates hair-like endings that are on our olfactory receptor cells inside the nose that electrical impulses carry through to the brain for us to process. Touch, we have many receptors in nerve cells that allow the sensation we feel by touch.

Mechanoreceptors provide the sensation of pushing and pulling within movement creating vibrations. Thermoreceptors provide the sensation of temperatures. Hearing, vibrations incoming from sound waves travel through the ear canal to reach the eardrum. The eardrum gives protection when there is impact. Vibrations then move three tiny bones in the middle of the ear that either amplify or increase the vibrations on their way to the cochlea which contains fluid for volume control.

Pitch is measured in hertz (Hz), loudness is measured in decibel (dB). Lower frequencies that are not in the range of are felt through our bodies as vibrations. Energy itself is matter that is made up of atoms and molecules that also creates a life source.

Energy causes atoms and molecules to always be in motion, either by bumping into each other or vibrating back and forth

The network inside our bodies communicates through vibrations as well as what surroundings our bodies are in contact with what their motion is. The motion of atoms and molecules creates two forms of energy, heat energy or thermal energy. Thermal energy is present in all matter. Everything that lives including us is made up of matter from atoms, molecules and energy. Motion itself is displacement, distances, velocity, acceleration, time and speed. Everything in the universe is moving in its own motion. However, energy is formed in every aspect of its own motion. What we feel, see, hear and touch" we receive the signals and respond to it in our own motion and time within our own bodies and senses.

We have to have everything communicated to ourselves, for ourselves to respond, whether to ourselves, others or surroundings. From "what we feel, see, hear and touch." What happens when we become thrown off within the motions, our responses are just as thrown off by what signals/triggers" we receive. The only way we individually can realize before we respond to mixed motion signals, whether physically or when they become emotional is to understand how we "ourselves" became confused.

When we realize confusion and apply understanding, communicating to ourselves and others becomes easy with respect. Physically becoming off balance with one sense with its ability being decreased, causes abilities from other senses to become off balance, having their abilities to perform increased. Over working other senses is what causes us to have inconveniences in tasks causing our frustration, from the loss of an ability of a sense, and the gain of other senses abilities. Our minds become confused on how it's responding to the body's attempt to adapt.

To those of us who struggle with any loss of the five senses can relate to the inconveniences of performing daily tasks. Becoming off balance with ourselves is when a sense's ability being decreased causes abilities from other senses to perform increased. Over working other senses is what causes us to have inconveniences in tasks causing our frustration. From the loss of an ability of a sense, our minds become confused on how it's responding to the body's attempt to adapt in a "time frame" we struggle to allow ourselves to adapt.

Time calculates the expectancy of energy that proves a source for atoms, cells and molecules to function. Displacement is the moving of something from its place or position.

Everything is always in motion displacement of our atoms and cells will always be happening over time. Speed and velocity either slow down the process or enhance all motion. Velocity is the speed of something given direction, acceleration is the ability to increase the rate or speed.

When certain things are moving too fast for us to comprehend and we don't take the time we need to process that it's natural and we can and will adapt, panic sets in.

When our panic sets in we then emotionally shut down that also affects our physical attempts. Our own energy that we used and provide for our own life source for our cells within our own bodies become drained with not having enough energy, the process of the speed velocity and time become slower.

We should all know that no matter how slow our healing process whether physically or mentally we do adapt because our life force wants to live and stay in motion. What we should all be concerned about is the time we give ourselves or lack of time we give ourselves.

Every aspect of anything that is alive has motion for movement, time and speed play a big role in all energy. We all know it takes time and energy to create cells to build muscles, our brain is one of the biggest muscles that creates and builds itself constantly giving us the ability to continue to learn and problem solve for survival.

The energy that we bring towards our mental versions that we process that is out Basic Sixth Sense is just as important as the energy we use to function within our physical health.

Everyone's health depends on each person's individual makeup, but all life sources needs within energy are all the same.

Most of the time our energy is restricted from what we bring to our mental health from conflicted by negative memories. When negative emotional energy overpowers our personality that we created to cope with what we can't understand we provide our lifestyle with dominances in power of negativity instead of demonstrating dominance of positivity that is needed.

When we don't allow ourselves time and understanding of the situation, and how time does has a big part in how frustrated and confused we would be lasting longer and increasing by the minute. Our minds become confused on the physical aspect of acceptances or non- acceptances. It is reasonable to believe that our minds can become confused on comprehending the mental aspect when analyzing our environments.

Recognizing our mind's ability is to perform communication in all forms as one of the basic senses rather than just recognizing the mind responses are only used towards triggers of the other five senses. Could allow us to recognize the full power of the mind and the effects it has. Acknowledging that the sense of the mind's communication and memories formed within communication would allow us to have the ability to comprehend all types of language, by mentally sensing levels of movement that are produced by all levels of physical appearances and elements.

As well as giving ourselves the memories needed to redirect and influence other memories for more appropriate communication.

When our minds become confused on the physical aspect of acceptances, it would be reasonable to believe that our minds can become confused on comprehending the mental aspect when analyzing our environments.

The basic five senses are used to focus on the physical aspect of environments. Environment is the appearance of objects around us. Situation's is the process of taking in details to reflect what movement is taking place in a moment. Therefor the basic five senses demonstrate the realization that the basic sixth sense would be of the mind's way of communicating, and the memories we require from how we communicate within what we recognize from all we have accepted. What we communicate to ourselves is all that we have chosen to recognize through over time.

What we recognize about how we communicate is what we remember to continue to communicate with. Having us respond accordingly to any situation we deem fit, whether it brings harm, discomfort or love and joy.

Recognizing is identifying something that has been previously encountered. Memory is our knowledge of experiences that stems from our thoughts on both, the physical aspects and mental procession that were created to form thoughts. Physical effects are what our body senses through our basic five senses. Mental procession is communication from what our mind senses with elements that are used to produce thoughts on physical surroundings and appearances.

Our basic sixth sense is all forms of communication we conduct, from any of our five senses to our mental procession to form thoughts, to our actions to communication within all forms due to our thoughts.

Our most amazing feature about our memory is having the ability to alter our memories within the same memory by taking a different approach to any situation if needed to "override" an old memory to create a new one. Giving us the abilities to have problem solving strategies or being able to correct ourselves and situations that are in need in any form of communication, every second of a moment we are communicating. Our constant problem-solving strategies are performed by us every miller second.

Whether it is happening within our bodies where we process it for being physically uncomfortable, or around us in elements where we disagree how things are. Becoming aware of having the ability of our basic sixth sense can allow in a time of a moment to alter our process of how we use our memory to change any outcomes successfully by how we communicate in every moment.

Every living organism uses memory to be able to recognize and evaluate their elements. Using senses repeatedly to determine if the elements have become slightly different over time. Life requires to follow changes in time's movements for growth to continue for survival, for all that lives. Just like all species we use the past to make movements in the present to provide for the future, that is nature.

Through advancements the invisible senses we use to recognize and use to respond become confused. Confusion causes chaos, Chaos is not a situation used in our senses of the basic five senses of natural needs to survive in being alive. Chaos is only in our basic sixth sense that determines how we live to just survive. In all honesty we all are like a code, if we align movements in the right form, we can break the code and move forward we have success in what we can achieve.

If we cannot break the code, we stay mentally in the same moment with only time from earth's rotation aging our bodies, limiting our mind's process within communication as we age. Causing confusion as we express our difficulty in communicating from lack of understanding ourselves.

Unlocking a part of our basic sixth sense to understand we will express confidence within the potential of improvements for a healthier lifestyle. Becoming aware of language of all types from verbal actions using sound waves for our sight and hearing in movement that creates what image we have in our memories, not just the physical actions we sense. That would allow us to recognize how we see communication and what it really means to us. Like a code, if we align movements in the right form, we can break the code and move forward.

PART TWO
Complete understanding how our Basic Sixth Sense is important.

Why the Basic Sixth Sense is important? It's important because once we are aware of a process we take notice, we understand, we apply it daily and we master the behavior individually and as a whole, eventually.

Contact with others is not avoidable! There is absolutely! no avoiding contact. Everything alive requires communication to live in a lifetime. In our style of communicating, we use many terms to breathe life into language. We have started the process as a whole in hopes that one day we could use the tools we invented to form within elementary to build progress over time as we are individually. With time passing in progress from intentions to apply knowledge and understanding.

I hope to help provide the beginning moments to advanced knowledge personally.

We use a categorize system to be able identify similarities to labels. Categorizing allows us to hold massive amounts of information in our memory. Terms are formed from meanings of what we know exists. Meanings are used to form information for us to understand terms. Labeling shortens the category systems we have created. If we do not know the correct terms to label with then we would categorize a meaning to a term wrongfully.

Terms can be the best and worst we use in trying to communicate our expressions. The best for describing being able to communicate civilly with great intentions.

The worst for describing a communication that would be uncivil with peaceful outcomes not included in intentions. Without our words, we feel weak, the stronger the word and meaning used. The stronger we express intentions of either being civilized or uncivilized. Uncivilized means impolite and bad mannered. Civilized means polite and well mannered. For an example applying meanings like ignorant, unwanted, misunderstood and worthless towards a person or oneself is the intention of not being civil.

Worthless is the meaning of having no real value. Unwanted is the meaning of no longer desired. Misunderstood is the meaning of failing to interpret or understand correctly.

Ignorant is the meaning of lacking knowledge or awareness in general, uneducated.

When harmful terms are used to amplify the situation responding civilly comes from understanding those harmful meanings are being used wrongfully. No human being should ever have terms applied to them that are made to be use as objects as material apparel.

Value's meaning is the regard that something is held to deserve, the importance, worth and usefulness. Deserve means having qualities worthy to be entitled to be good enough. Importance means the state of being of great significance.

Useful meaning is the quality of having utility, especially practical worth or applicability. The meaning of desired is strongly wished for and intended. Intended means planned or meant.

Diminishing other persons value and usefulness to provide that appearance of worthlessness within that person.

Understanding meaning is perceived as the intended meaning of a word and language. If our own choice of words is not chosen correctly, the response we will receive back will not be what we want to receive both to ourselves and others.

Once applied and wrongfully use of the terms within meanings like no value, not desired, mentally uneducated are included in a form of aggression only creates nothing to be valuable for desire to not be applied and uneducated moments from becoming ill mentally.

Pointing out what is being misunderstood comes from what doesn't want to be understood. Therefor our knowledge of growth ceases for the moment in time. It's a faster process of growth when we attempt that we must adapt to a new communication style. Because pointing out ignorance only disables learning. Pointing out unwanted only brings confusion to what is wanted.

Logic is literal in communication, when speaking we search for the literal meaning behind every statement so we can comprehend someone's reasoning. If the meaning is causing confusion, then we will be confused on how to respond.

What we interrupt from someone's response that shows signs of them lacking in their own judgement should not be expressed by ourselves, it is not our place to influence them. Influencing them to understand only our reasoning will just cause other problems. Especially when your reasoning needs to be adjusted to the situation as a whole and not by what your prescriptive is alone.

We should never intrude in the moment when they are processing their own sense of mind. To be able to get a better understanding of what is to be expected within their own personal surroundings.

Everyone has responses to every action that is taken regardless of if there is not enough time in the moment to gather all thoughts to make every word make sense.

In a crossfire with no time in allowing anyone to use their own sense of mind confusion happens. Not being able to understand something causes more confusion that will take the process on how to figure out longer than needed.

For us not to discover who we are and where we stand amongst those who are different is not hurting those who influenced us, it's only hurting ourselves. Our sense of who we are, how we think and how we form our memories.

This will help to notice the differences to form our own opinion that will help us evolve our emotions, that would react best to the differences we encounter.

There are many ways of communication, but we must keep in mind they are invented to do one job and that's to communicate how we live our life.

How we live our Life! When communicating go's bad We all share the same capabilities of communicating no matter the amount of difficulties we experience. Weather the difficulties stem from the basic five senses becoming lost and reprogramming others to communicate bringing frustration.

Or the difficulties within the basic sixth sense "within memories" that have not been properly noticed to be used and have become replaced by impulses to carry out acts within a moment instead of planning-out what we truly want to be expressed.

To be able to identify difficulties in communicating can be reviewed by the amount of frustration and inconvenience of expressing an emotion in the attempts to communicate, whether it being anger or being intimate or being saddened.

If we believe we have been communicating properly because we have become used to the same reaction we got. That would continue to allow us to continue to respond with the inconvenience with anger, intimation and sadness.

If communicating properly is done right there wouldn't be frustration, inconvenience or becoming overwhelmed while there is communication. Because those emotions we feel only presents itself when there are indeed difficulties, we experience communicating to ourselves while expressing amongst others as well. We share the reasonability that comes with communication all together, ourselves and others.

We cannot fully understand our value or the value of life and survival if communicating properly was not introduced to us at an early age. Not getting the knowledge of intercepting correctly and responding appropriately would allow us as adults to become angry with whom we feel isn't taking responsibility for their own actions.

Anger steaming from intercepting actions by others who give us a feeling of them lacking in securing our comfort while being around them, causing overwhelming emotions separating them from our personal lives and associating them with just being a part of the life we live with no personal connection. But those actions we take upon other people are only the actions we can upon ourselves.

We aren't securing our comfort, we aren't intercepting our own actions, we separate from ourselves.

Textbook definition of responsibility is "The state or fact of having a duty to deal with or control over someone". To describe a feeling of someone who is or isn't participating in only the view of our opinion is just a form of be-littering. One person can't handle more than one task alone and it is unfair to describe the parts they lack in being irresponsible.

We all share the same responsibility on how someone acts out from repercussions of being mistreated and how we act out from mistreating ourselves.

If we take away someone's will-power to stay sane by using words to empower them they will act out in anger, if we do the same to ourselves, we act out in anger.

Difficulties in communication bring out the anger, intimidation and sadness that forms physical and mental health issues with.

Anger can eventually cause harm to different systems of the body. Our brain shunts blood away from the gut and towards muscles for preparation for physical exertion, causing heart rate, blood pressure, respiration and body temperature to increase and the mind becomes focused.

Health problems include headaches, digestion issues, insomnia, high blood pressure, heart attack and stroke.

When we are sad the chemicals called opioids increase inflammatory proteins in our blood that attack our immune system. Our minds and bodies respond with a cold or flu affect. When we become intimidated, we are fearful. The adrenaline that is released is carried through the bloodstream. Affecting the autonomic nervous system.

The autonomous nervous system controls our heart rate, dilation of our pupils and our sweat and saliva glades. Rapid heart rate, "tachycardia", affects our bodies by depriving oxygen to your organs and tissues. By the inability to have our heart pump blood effectively when our hearts are beating too fast. Causing shortness of breath, lightheadedness, chest pain, fainting and rapid pulse. Which are dangerous and could cause strokes, heart attacks or sudden death.

The amount of sweat and saliva released would be the amount of dehydration we allow ourselves to have, if we don't replace the amount of fluid leaving our bodies. The effects we get with dehydration are dry mouth, tiredness, headache, dizziness or lightheadedness and minimal urine. Dilation of our pupils causes vision to become blurry.

Blurry vision gives the inability to see fine details. Upon not being able to see fine details we would require headache, migraines and light sensitivity. too much of anything we put in our bodies allows the reaction it produces to become off balanced.

The difference between appropriate and inappropriate forms of communication, is how we associate to ourselves why it would be important that our bodies must go through those changes from reactions. Our bodies react regardless of if we have control or no control. If we don't have control neither does our bodies.

Naturally we have these chemicals with their balance. Too much uncontrolled reactions released into our bodies from moments we can control does not allow us to improve our mental and physical health. We were designed to have control of our environments through all our senses that are provided at birth, regardless of what areas within all our senses that we wouldn't be able to control.

Different types of control is found in other ways to balance out living from birth. Controlling ourselves in every aspect is what we were born to do, and what cannot be controlled we try to find control. Controlling harmful situations need to be communicated to ourselves, to be able to address what is important for health and what is harmful for health.

Health is the meaning of well-being, the state of being free from illness or injury. We really can't be free, but we can control.

Harmful is the meaning of causing or what would be likely to cause harm that could bring damage, to all senses. Preventing harm to the health of ourselves and others is what is important. Prevents meaning is to keep something from happening or arising. The meaning of important is, great significance or value that is likely to have a profound effect on success, survival and well-being. The lesson to be learned is how important it is to control commutation to prevent anything that is harmful, not just to all our senses but the senses of others.

PART THREE

To apply our Basic Sixth Sense

How to live life with our Basic Sixth Sense to gain the control of communication, is to have complete understanding. To understand that no matter what type of trauma we have indoored in our past, by others who did not communicate rightfully with us. It does not make our personally.

What makes our personally is by how we perceive the miss- communication and by what we self-taught ourselves to cope. This important information can allow us to re-teach ourselves, and others in how we understand, bringing confidence in accepting everything we could not accept before. Start to listen closely to the words you say at every moment you speak, hear each note within the sound of your tone when displayed.

Become aware of all the different types of frequencies that represent your tone. Our hearing is most sensitive in the 2000-5000 Hz frequency rage, raging in our comfort levels.

Start paying attention to the moments within events that have a different pace while expressing your tones. Tempo is the rate or speed of motion producing pace. Realizing if the tempo within other people around you becomes overwhelming that allows your tone that is within your own voice to become off balance while you speak. Sensing your own tones and why you express them will allow you to take notice and correct yourself for a more calming choice within words to use and redirect other tones to follow the same pace.

Pay close attention to each word that you use that represents your vocabulary. Allow yourself to become aware if you are using the correct terms within the choice of wording you use to describe your actions. If the term does not match up to the word while describing, replace your word and educate yourself on what words have true meaning towards all actions you take into your vocabulary.

Your vocabulary is important in communicating properly. Allow yourself to express who you are with how you speak. Allow yourself to use your sense within touch to feel your own movements while you move.

Feel how you physically show your excitement. Feel how you physically show how you lose your interest. Start to take notice to every touch you feel within every vibration against your skin.

Notice the different pressures or disgust you feel within yourself from your body's endorsements. Allow yourself to feel temperatures and textures within every vibration that's produced within objects to feel your serotonin levels rise and continue with that happiness.

Take notice in all the different odors when you inhale, notice the pleasures or discomfort the odors bring to you. Begin to re-distinguish every distinct flavor that intrigues or disgusts you. It takes only a small number of seconds within minutes each day to catch and take notice of details in rediscovering who you are to not allow them to be forgotten and insert those details into your daily routines. The opportunely you get when close examining yourself is the control you allow yourself now to have.

The self-control remains in the rest of seconds that you took out of your minutes to discover who you are. The control that is allowed, will act out upon what you smell, touch, hear, see, taste and now sense. The control within the reasoning on why and how it's learned will provide the reasons why any moment before would distinguish of impulses in decision making.

Last, but not least in discovering what you're capable of when you're in control, understanding your own memories and why it brings impulses when controlling is not embraced. Your memories take part in decisions that have been created from the past. Even right now, because of tomorrow today is now the past and in this moment, you have already created a new memory for tomorrow. Either of approval or disapproval you cannot deny that my words are now not your memories.

This moment is exactly why the past can be explained and the future can be corrected. Introducing a different outlook on how to control your experiences will have you moving forward tomorrow from anything uncomfortable today and yesterday brought.

We can either make tomorrow better or worse. The world's problems begin with everyone's personal problem. The moment our race began to create communication amongst us all with words is the moment we begun to miss use them. Creating controversy and struggles in every category.

The categories you personally struggle with will dissipate when you allow yourself to focus within your basic sixth sense, balance yourself by getting to know the science behind yourself. Everyday you will continue to learn and provide yourself and others the opportunity too.

May you all use an X to symbolize noticing what is wrong. May you all put a line running across the middle of the X symbolizing you are correcting what's wrong. May you all put a line running up and down to symbolize it's corrected. May all the positive + always cross over all the negative x mistakes. May you all have peace, love and happiness within yourselves and others. May you all understand the power of healthy energy and the worth in feeding it inside each and every one of you. May your understanding of the Basic Sixth Sense provide you the reasonings to fix what needs to be fixed.

This book is written from every memorable moment good and bad, and the correcting that took place from inside because of them. The dedication to knowledge and understanding reasoning is to provide the correct guide for my family and loved ones and the world individually, and as a whole

I dedicate this book and all the progress from the process that will follow to my children. Whom will provide the world their own guidance and knowledge to the world and their offspring by the practice of what is learned to teach.